Mathematics
Skills

Exercises devised by David Kirkby
a senior lecturer in Mathematics Education at
Sheffield Hallam University
Illustrated by John Haslam

Learning Rewards is a home-learning programme designed to help your child succeed at school with the National Curriculum. It has been extensively researched with parents and teachers.

This book, *Mathematics Skills*, and its companion title, *Mathematics Practice*, cover important aspects of the National Curriculum at Key Stage I.

Children should start with the *Skills* books (with younger children this is important) and progress to the *Practice* books.

The *Skills* book teaches basic skills and new concepts through structured and enjoyable activities. The *Practice* book reinforces and builds on these skills by the essential repetition of exercises.

You will need to work through each page with your child and talk about what is required. The content is progressive, so start from the front of the book.

The fold-out progress chart is a useful record of your child's performance. Always reward your child's work with encouragement and a gold star sticker.

When you come to the end of the book you will find a fun, wipe-clean learning game.

Key to symbols on the page:

 skills covered by each exercise as they relate to the National Curriculum

 notes for parents, explaining specific teaching points

 follow-up activities which will extend your child's understanding of the exercise

series editor: Nina Filipek
series designer: Paul Dronsfield
Copyright © 1996 World International Limited.
All rights reserved.
Published in Great Britain by
World International Limited, Deanway Technology Centre,
Wilmslow Road, Handforth, Cheshire SK9 3FB.
Printed in Italy.
ISBN 0 7498 2706 8

Mathematics

Counting to 10

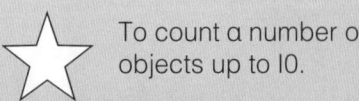 To count a number of objects up to 10.

Count the rabbits in each group.   Write the number.

☐ rabbits

☐ rabbits

☐ rabbits

☐ rabbits

Mathematics

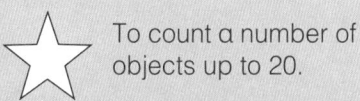

To count a number of objects up to 20.

Counting to 20

Count the number of each fruit.   Write the number.

apples

pears

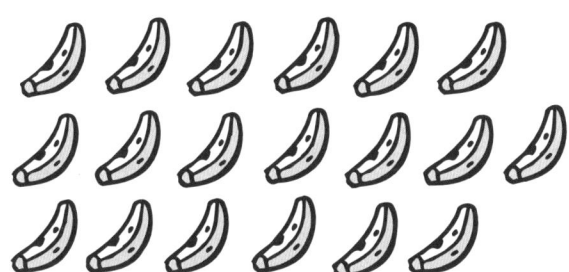

bananas

plums

 Look for things to count in the home, e.g. buttons, building bricks, or sweets.

3

Mathematics

Ordering

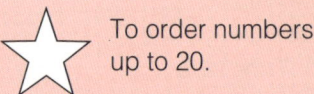
To order numbers up to 20.

Write the missing numbers on each snake.

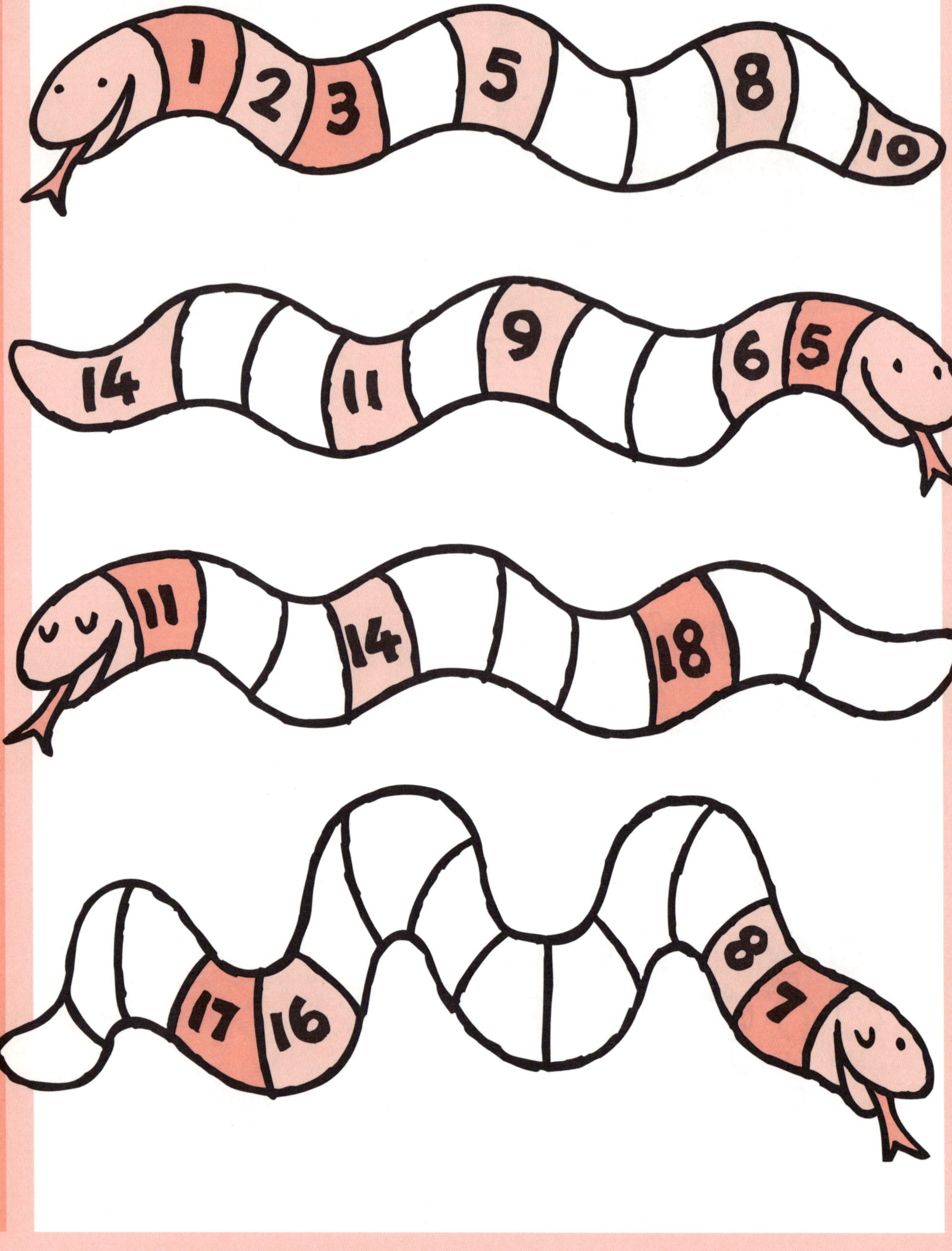

Mathematics

 To locate position on a number line (up to 20).

Number lines

Join each kite to its position on the line.

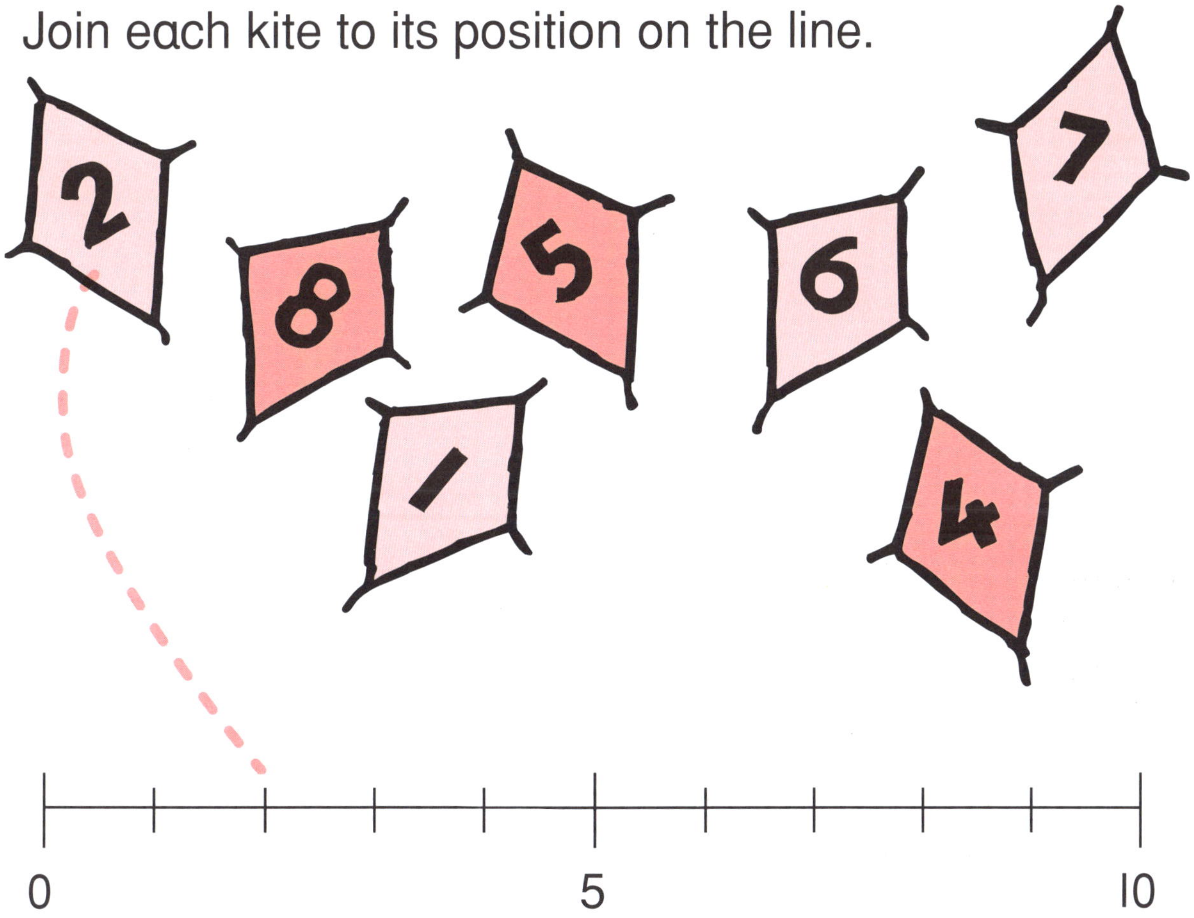

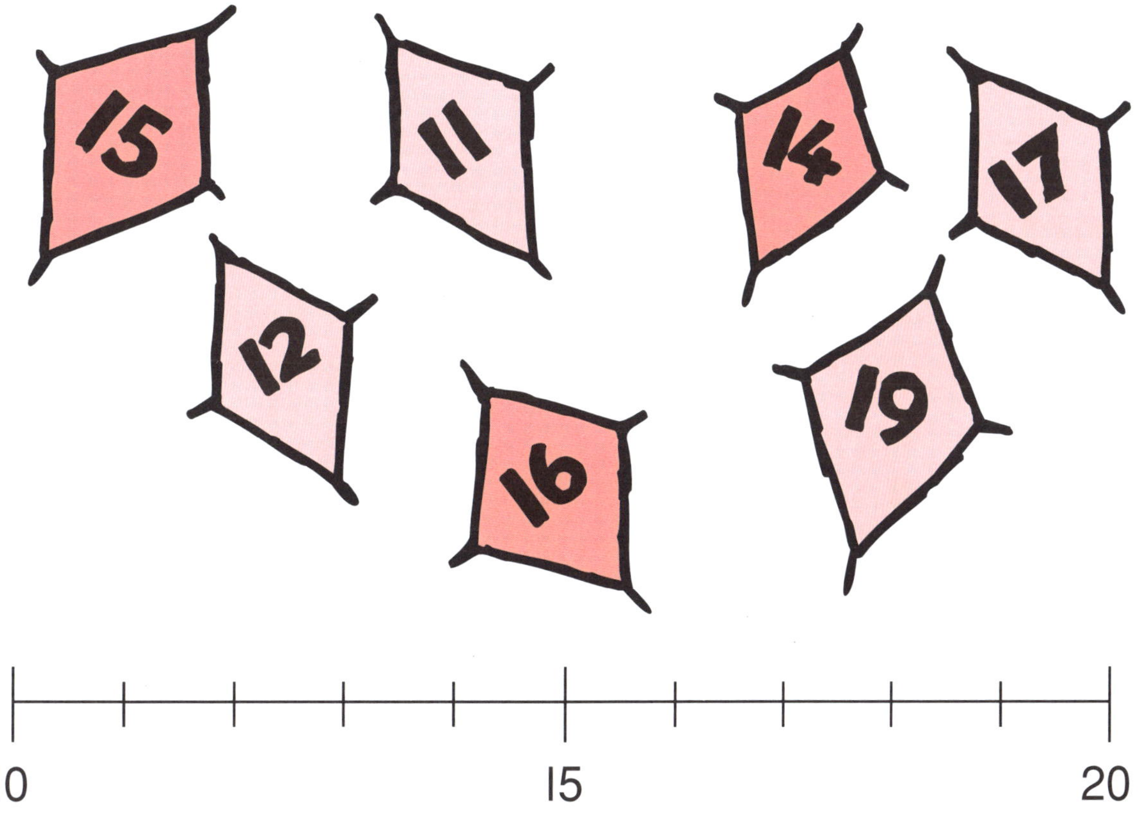

Mathematics

Time: o'clock

 To read the time (o'clocks) on analogue and digital clocks.

Write the time under each clock.

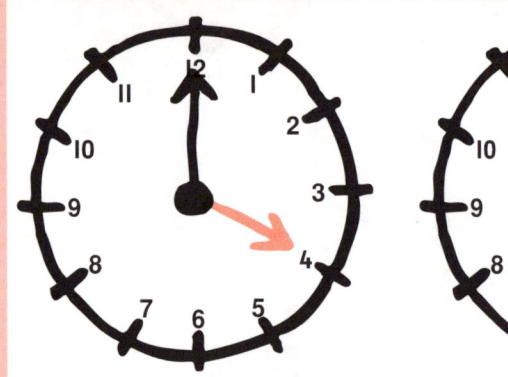
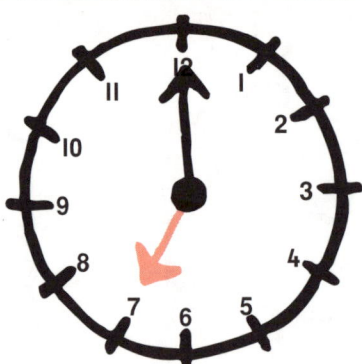
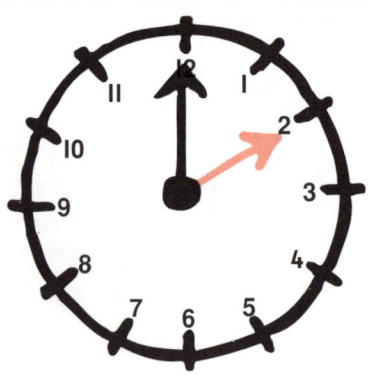

4 o'clock

1.00   10.00   6.00

Make the clocks show these times:

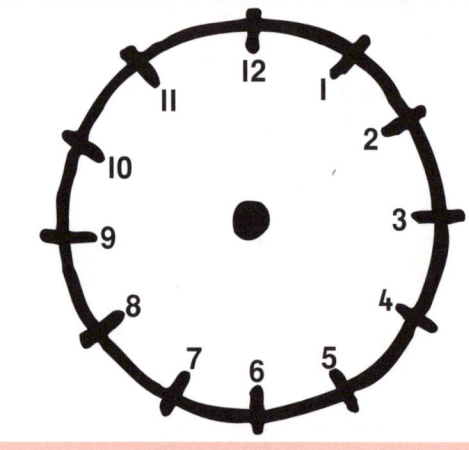
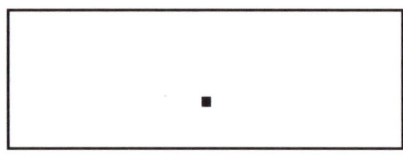

8 o'clock   11 o'clock

6

Mathematics

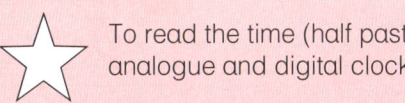
To read the time (half past) on analogue and digital clocks.

Time: half past

Write the time under each clock.

half past 2

1.30   5.30   11.30

Make the clocks show these times:

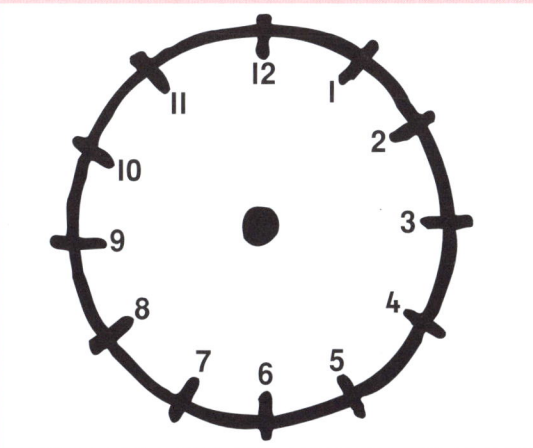

half past 8

half past 9

Point out that the hour hand is half-way between the numbers.

7

Mathematics

Tallest and shortest

To recognise the tallest and shortest of a set of heights.

Ann   Tom   Greg   Ayub

_____ is tallest   _____ is shortest

tree   house   bus   flagpole

_____ is tallest   _____ is shortest

Mathematics

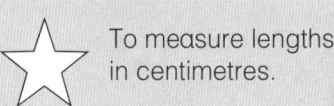
To measure lengths in centimetres.

Measuring with centimetres

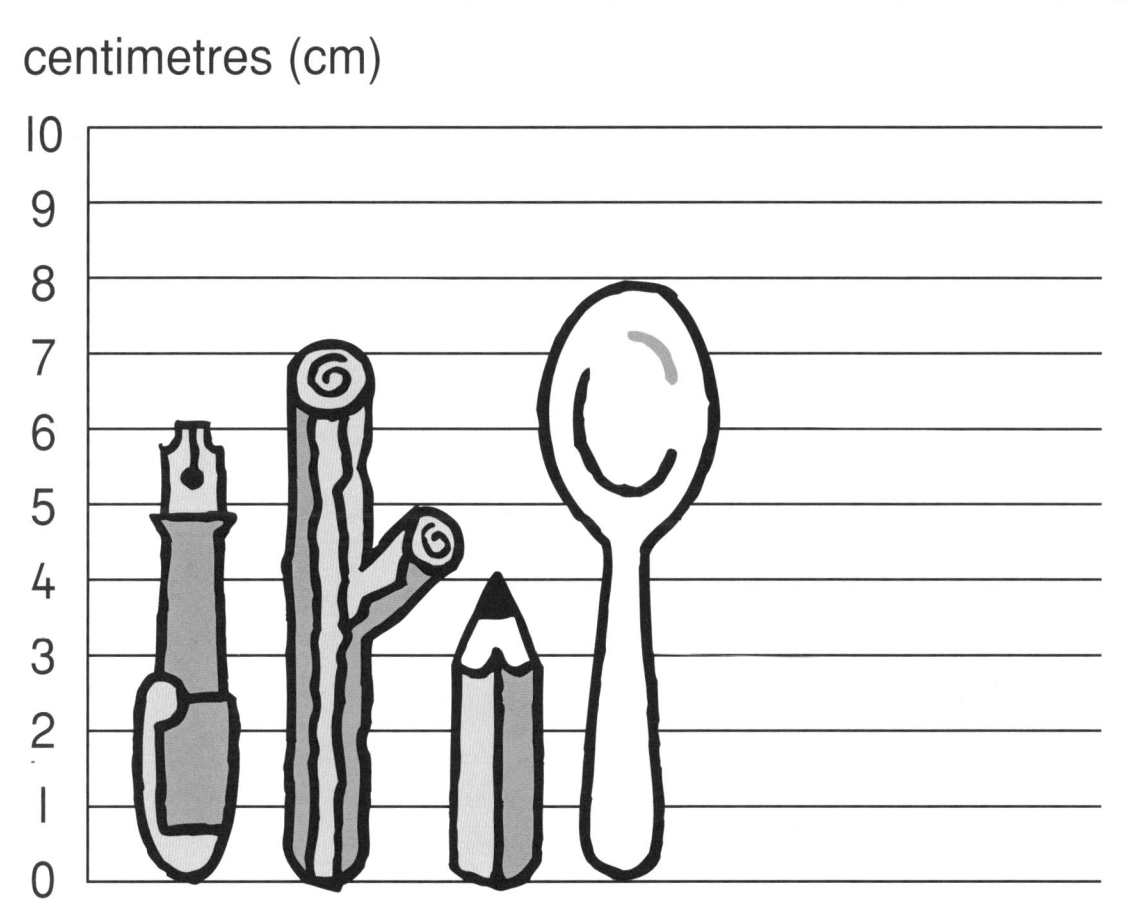

centimetres (cm)

Write the length of these objects:

pen ☐ cm   pencil ☐ cm

stick ☐ cm   spoon ☐ cm

Which is the longest? ☐   Which is the shortest? ☐

Next to the spoon draw another pencil which is 5cm long, and another pen which is 9cm long.

 Make sure your child can use a ruler accurately. Then look for things to measure in the home.

9

Mathematics

Money

To recognise relationships between coins (1p, 2p, 5p, 10p).

Join two coins to match each price.
Each coin can only be joined once.

7p   11p   15p

3p   12p   6p

Mathematics

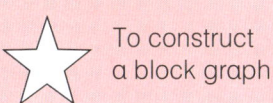 To construct a block graph.

Block graph

Colour blocks, from the bottom upwards, to show how many there are of each creature.

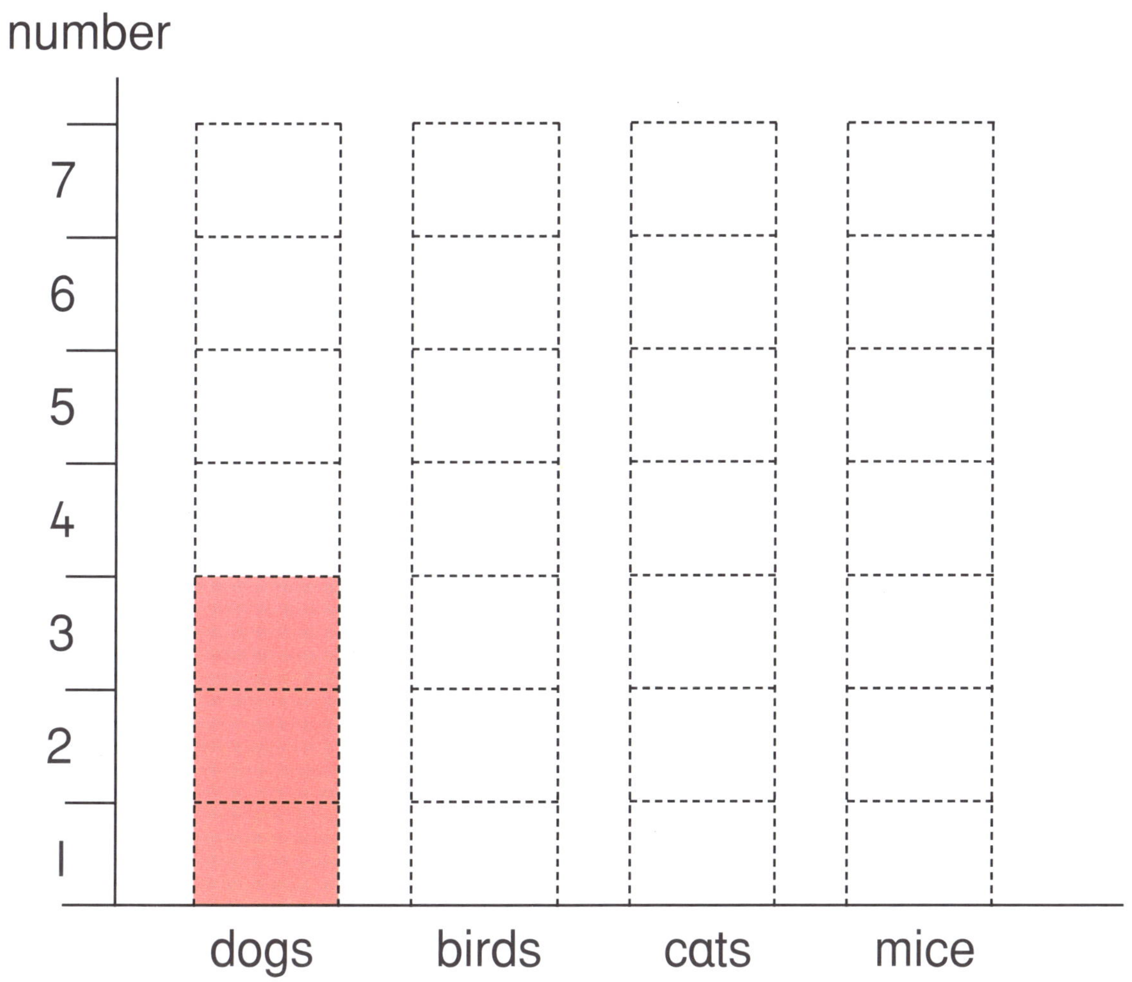

number

7				
6				
5				
4				
3				
2				
1				
	dogs	birds	cats	mice

11

Mathematics

Tens and units

 To recognise the relationship between tens and units.

Write the number of cubes each time.

tens   units

| 3 | 2 |

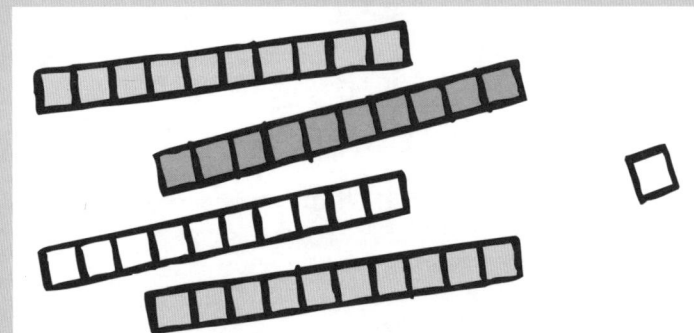

tens   units

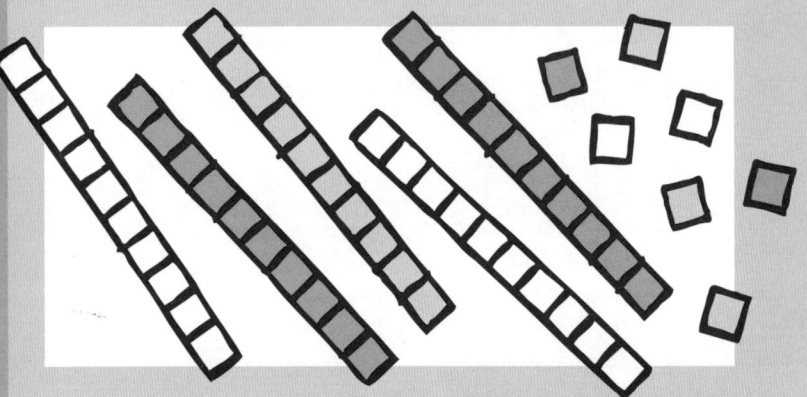

tens   units

Draw the cubes for this number:

tens   units

| 2 | 5 |

Mathematics

Tens and units

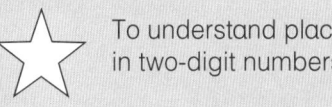
To understand place-value in two-digit numbers.

Write the number shown on each abacus.

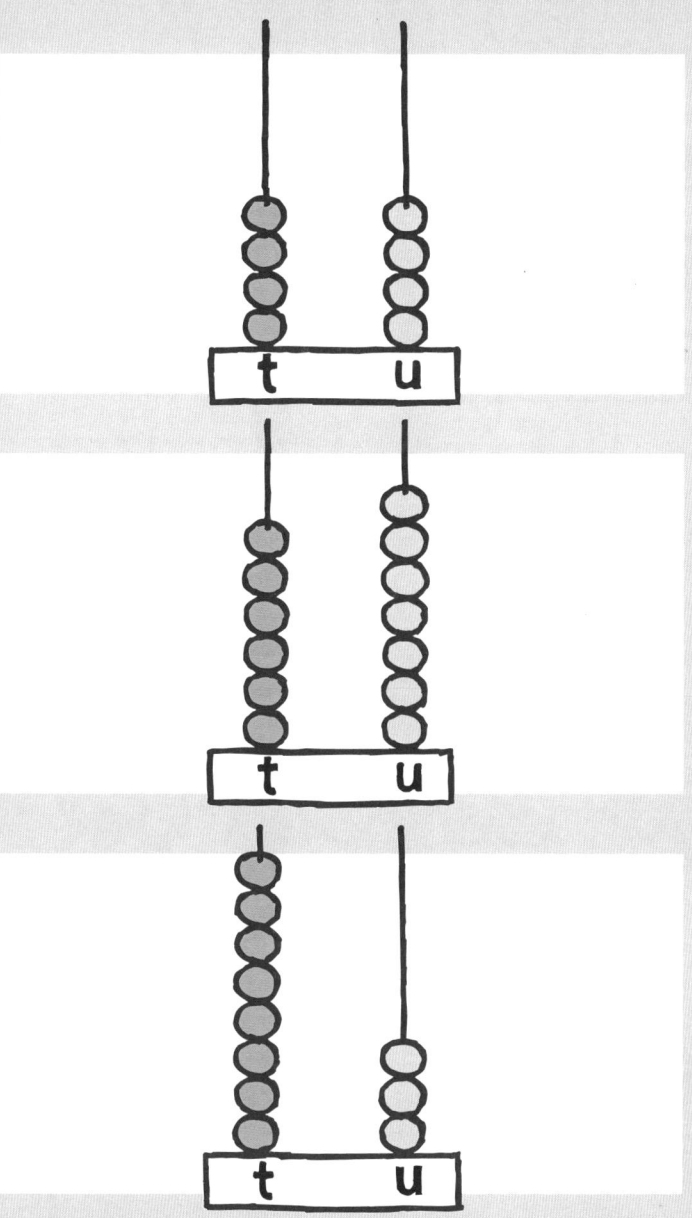

tens   units

| 4 | 4 |

tens   units

tens   units

Draw the beads for this abacus:

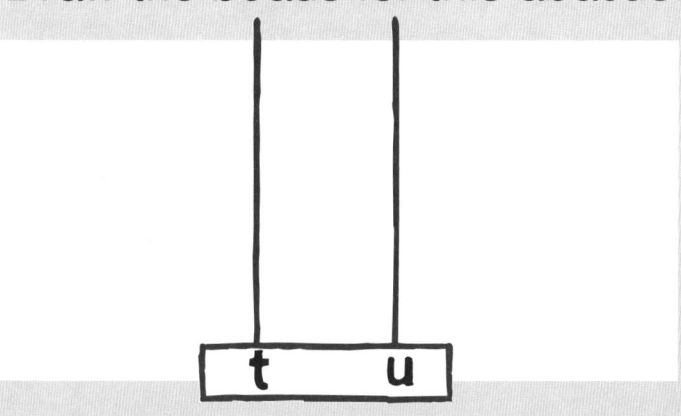

tens   units

| 5 | 6 |

13

Mathematics

2-digit numbers

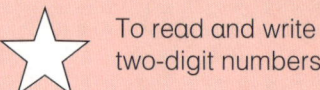
To read and write two-digit numbers.

Write the missing numbers on the trains.

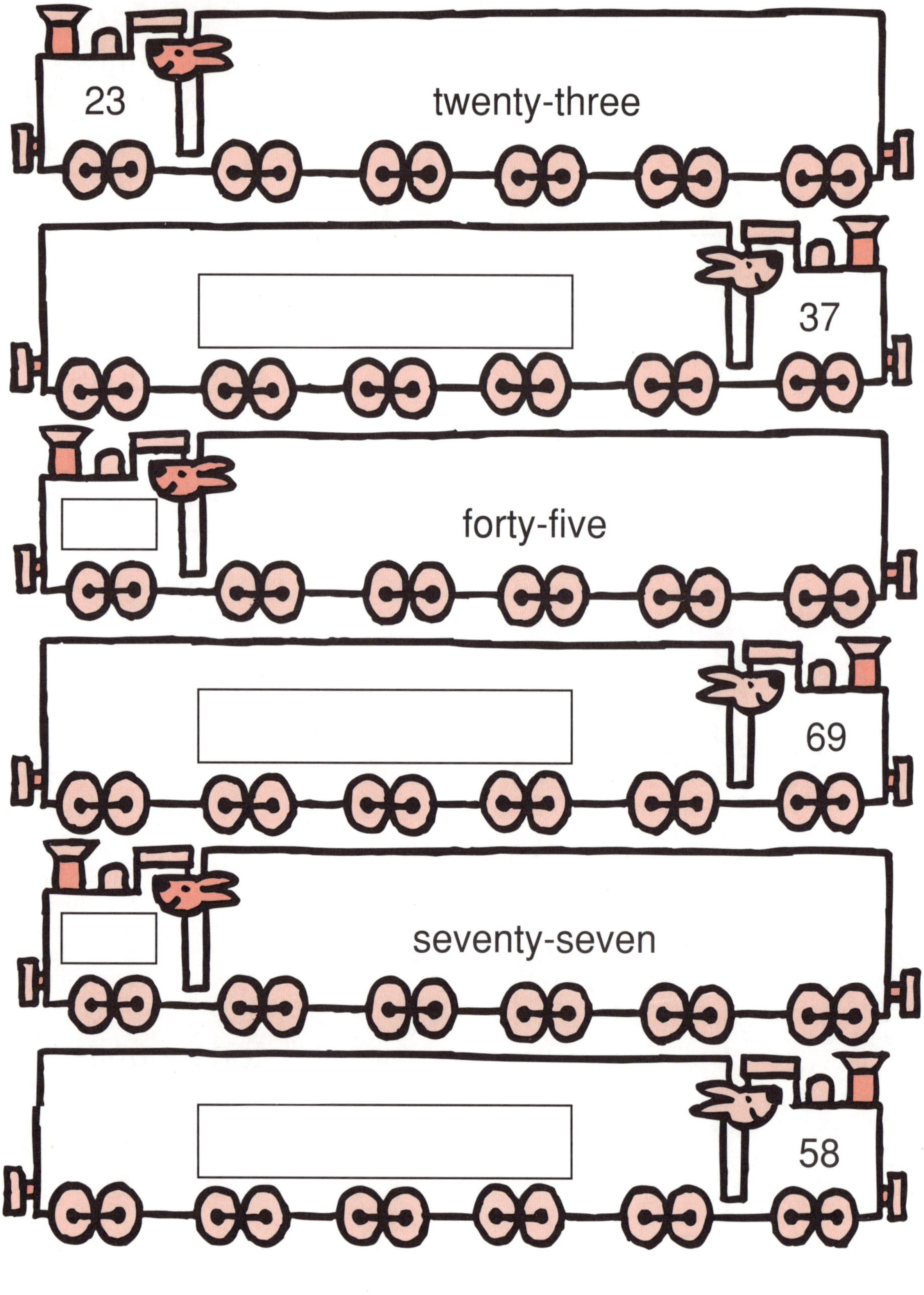

23   twenty-three

[   ]   37

[   ]   forty-five

[   ]   69

[   ]   seventy-seven

[   ]   58

Mathematics

 To recognise and name squares, circles, rectangles and triangles.

Shapes

Colour the shapes:

red	green	yellow	blue
squares	rectangles	circles	triangles

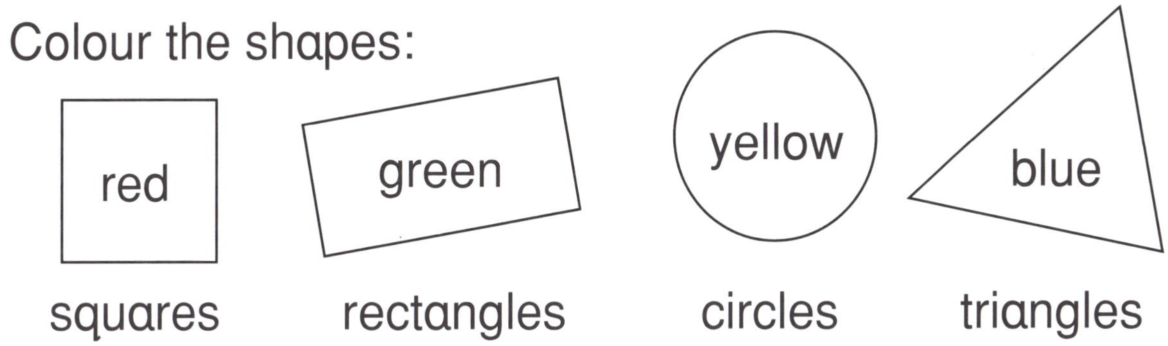

Draw one more triangle and colour it.

Cut these shapes out of card or sticky paper and make pictures with them.

Mathematics

Shapes

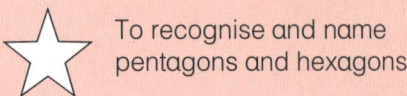
To recognise and name pentagons and hexagons.

Colour the shapes:

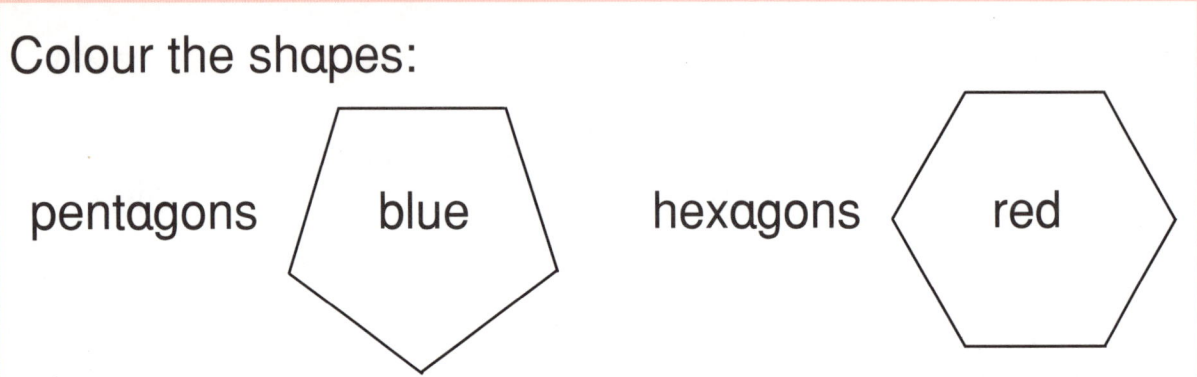

pentagons — blue   hexagons — red

Draw one more pentagon and colour it.

16

Mathematics

Halves and quarters

To recognise one half and one quarter of a shape.

Colour one half of each shape.

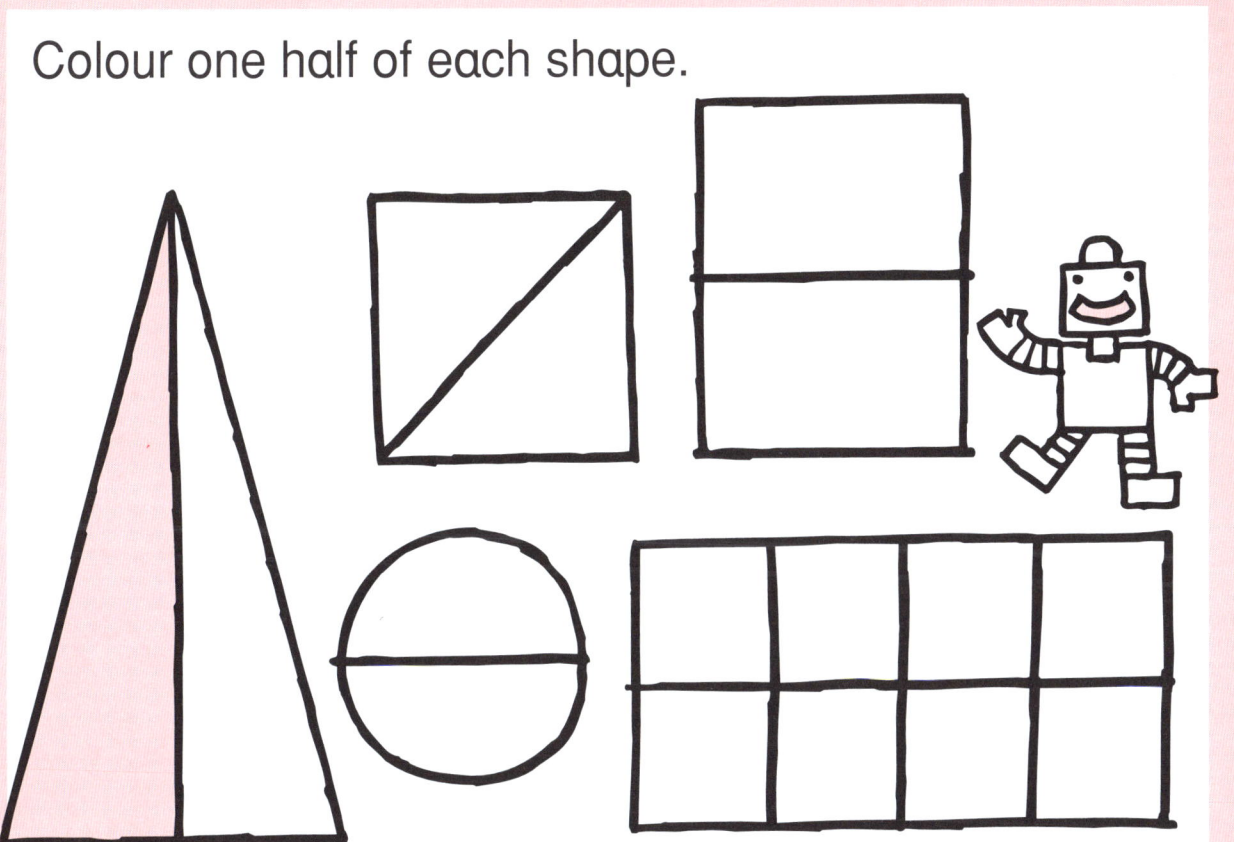

Colour one quarter of each shape.

Cut cakes, chocolate bars, or biscuits into halves and quarters.

17

Mathematics

Odds and evens

 To recognise odd and even numbers.

Colour the odd numbers pink.

| 1 | 2 | 3 | 4 | 5 | 6 | 7 | 8 | 9 | 10 |

1	2	3	4	5	6	7
8	9	10	11	12	13	14
15	16	17	18	19	20	21
22	23	24	25	26	27	28
29	30	31	32	33	34	35
36	37	38	39	40	41	42
43	44	45	46	47	48	49

Colour the even numbers pink.

| 1 | 2 | 3 | 4 | 5 | 6 | 7 | 8 | 9 | 10 |

1	2	3	4	5	6	7	8	9	10
11	12	13	14	15	16	17	18	19	20
21	22	23	24	25	26	27	28	29	30
31	32	33	34	35	36	37	38	39	40
41	42	43	44	45	46	47	48	49	50
51	52	53	54	55	56	57	58	59	60

Mathematics

 To recognise the relationship between hundreds, tens and units.

Hundreds, tens and units

Write the number of cubes each time.

hundreds	tens	units
2	3	5

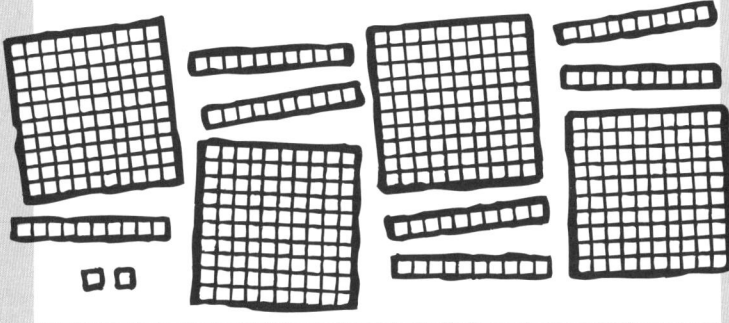

hundreds	tens	units

hundreds	tens	units

Draw the cubes for this number:

hundreds	tens	units
1	4	3

19

Mathematics

Hundreds, tens and units

To understand place-value in three-digit numbers

Write the number shown on each abacus.

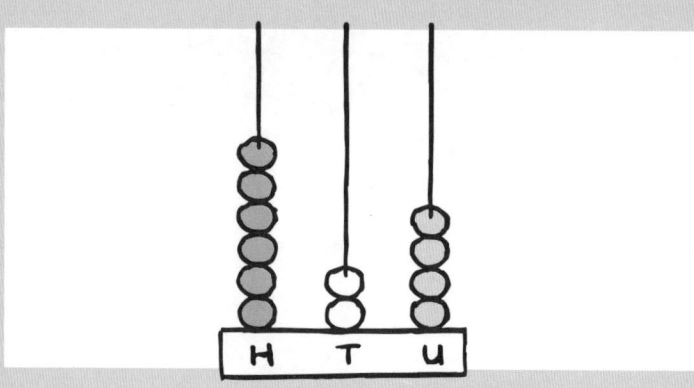

hundreds tens units

6   2   4

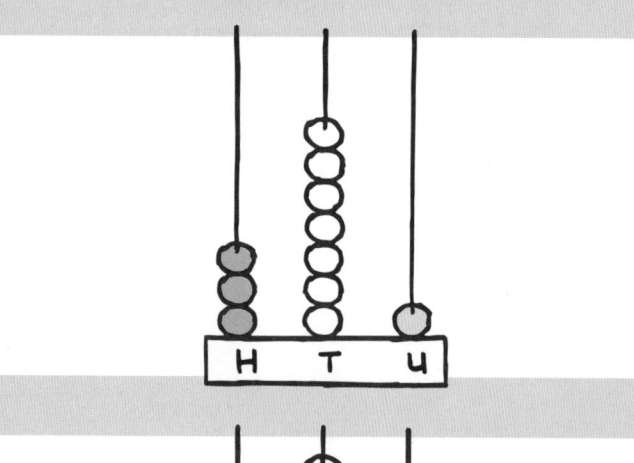

hundreds tens units

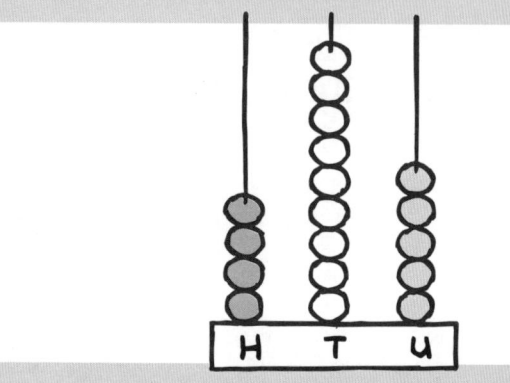

hundreds tens units

Draw the beads for this abacus:

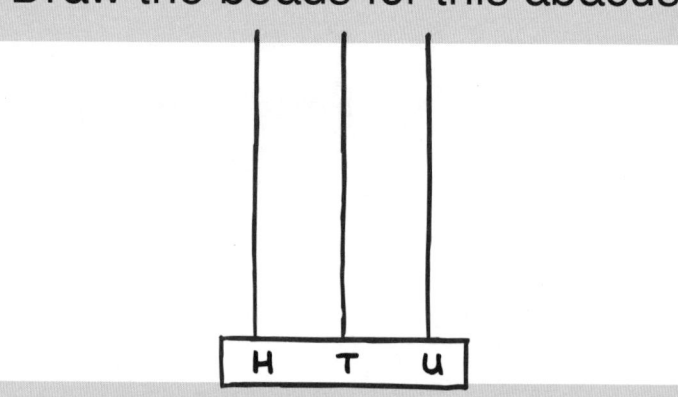

hundreds tens units

2   5   7

Mathematics

 To read and write three-digit numbers.

Three-digit numbers

Write the missing numbers on the trains.

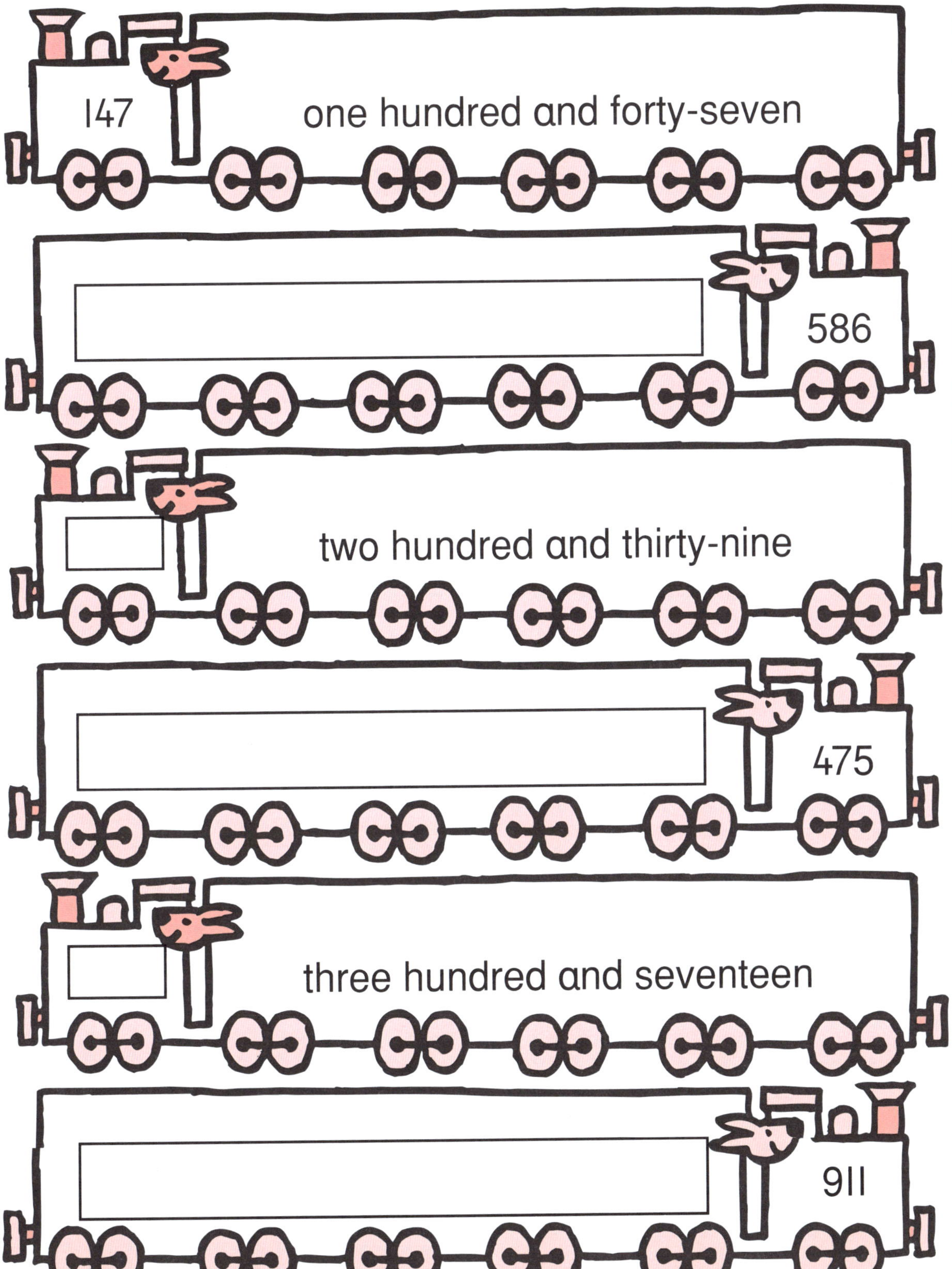

147 — one hundred and forty-seven

___ — 586

___ — two hundred and thirty-nine

___ — 475

___ — three hundred and seventeen

___ — 911

Mathematics

Tallies

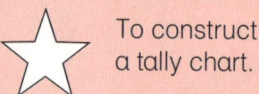

To construct a tally chart.

Football results

Strikers	2	City	1
Sparrows	0	Racers	2
Blues	0	Potters	0
United	1	Bees	0
Leopards	2	Yellows	1
Jugglers	3	Seagulls	3
Kickers	4	Lions	2
Athletic	1	Panthers	5
Falcons	0	Town	1
Cockatoos	4	Fowlers	1
Reds	1	Buzzers	1
Tigers	2	Whites	1
Hornets	3	Stripes	2
Rovers	4	Hoops	0
Eagles	0	Toddlers	1
Wasps	3	Canaries	0

Eight teams scored 0 goals.
Complete the tally chart to see how many teams scored 1, 2, 3, 4 and 5 goals.

Goals	Tallies	Totals
0	⊮⊮ |||	8
1		
2		
3		
4		
5		

22

Mathematics

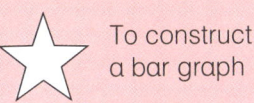 To construct a bar graph

Bar graph

Draw a bar to show how many cards there are in each suit. The first bar has been done for you.

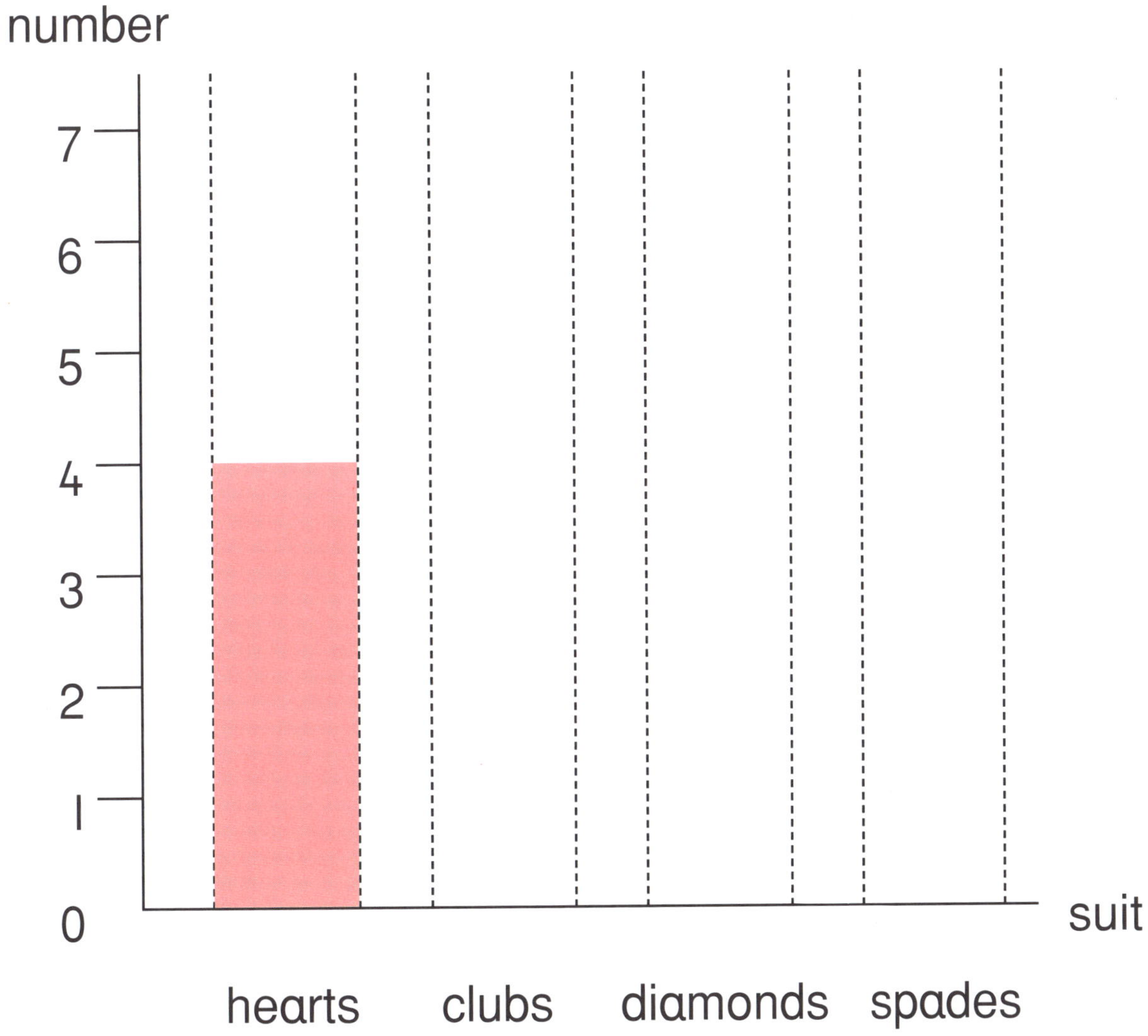

number

7
6
5
4
3
2
1
0

hearts   clubs   diamonds   spades   suit

most   least

23

Mathematics

Halves

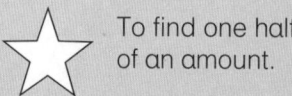 To find one half of an amount.

Loop one half of each set.

   one half of 6 is 3

   one half of ☐ is ☐

   one half of ☐ is ☐

   one half of ☐ is ☐

   one half of ☐ is ☐

   one half of ☐ is ☐

   one half of ☐ is ☐

Mathematics

Quarters

★ To find one quarter of an amount.

Loop one quarter of each set.

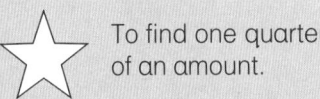 one quarter of 8 is 2

 one quarter of ☐ is ☐

 one quarter of ☐ is ☐

 one quarter of ☐ is ☐

 one quarter of ☐ is ☐

one quarter of ☐ is ☐

25

Mathematics

Time: quarter past, quarter to

 To read the time (quarter past, quarter to) on analogue and digital clocks.

Write the time under each clock.

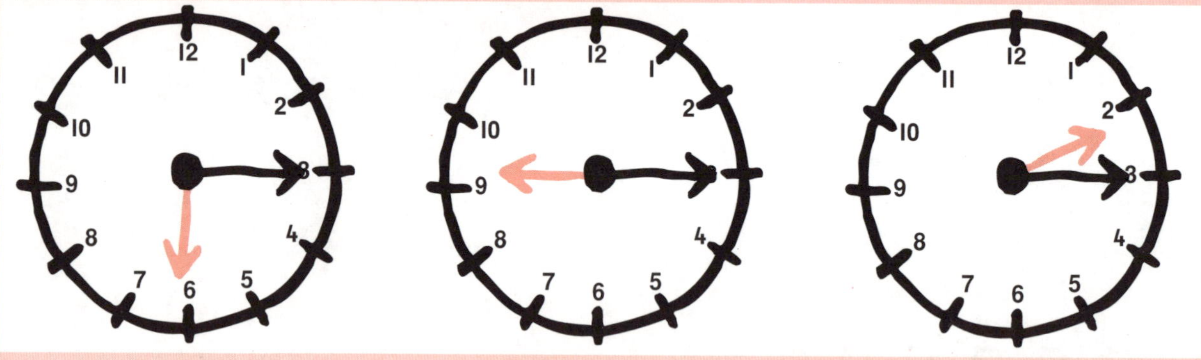

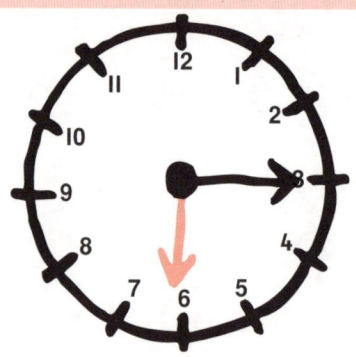

quarter past 6		

4.15	8.15	10.15

Write the time under each clock.

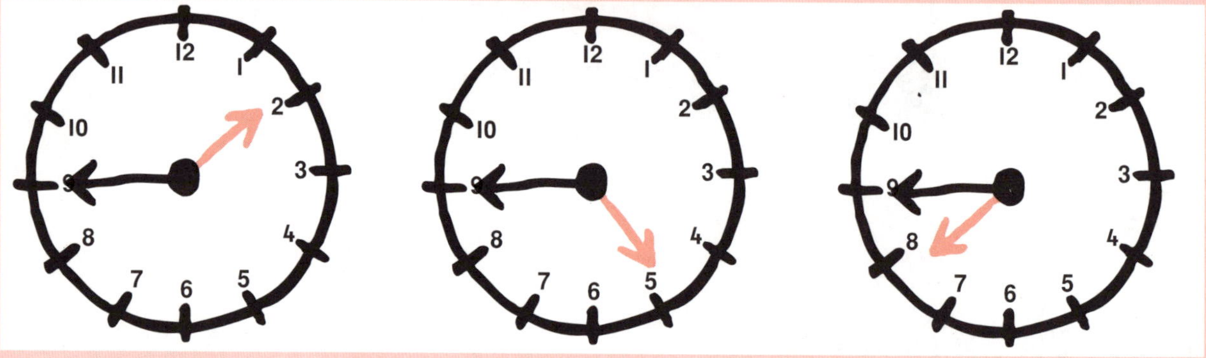

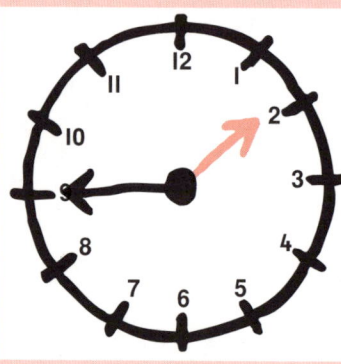

quarter to 2		

2.45	6.45	11.45

26

Mathematics

 To read the time (five minute intervals) on analogue and digital clocks.

Time: five minutes

Write the time under each clock.

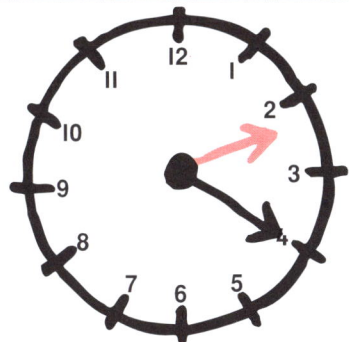 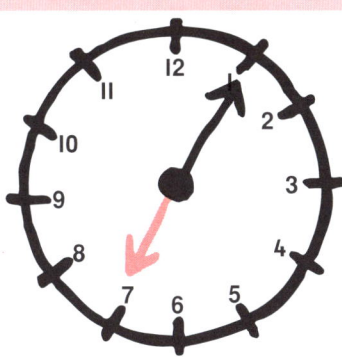 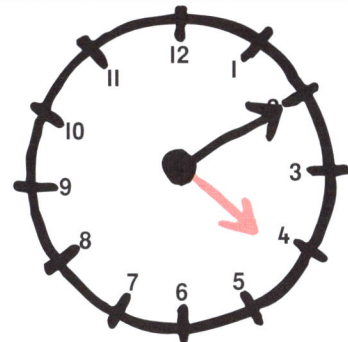

| 20 past 2 | | |

| 3.05 | 10.25 | 6.20 |

| | | |

Write the time under each clock.

 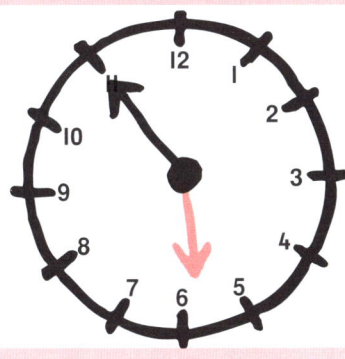 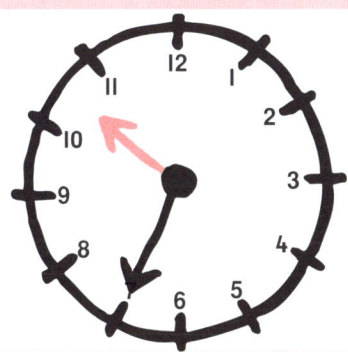

| 20 to 4 | | |

| 9.50 | 11.35 | |

 Time is a difficult concept to grasp. If younger children find these exercises difficult, you can always come back to them later.

27

Mathematics

Money

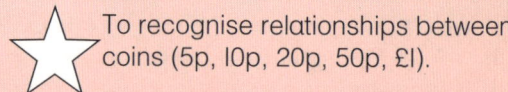
To recognise relationships between coins (5p, 10p, 20p, 50p, £1).

Join two coins to match each price.
Each coin can only be joined once.

You can practise this activity using real money.

28

Mathematics

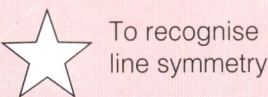 To recognise line symmetry

Symmetry

This picture is symmetrical. If it is folded at the line, one half fits exactly on to the other half.

Draw the other half of these symmetrical pictures.

 Point to things in the home that are symmetrical, e.g. chairs, tables, clothes.

 Make symmetrical pictures by using thick paints and folding the paper over.

29

Mathematics

Number lines

 To locate position on a number line (up to 200).

Join each kite to its position on the line.

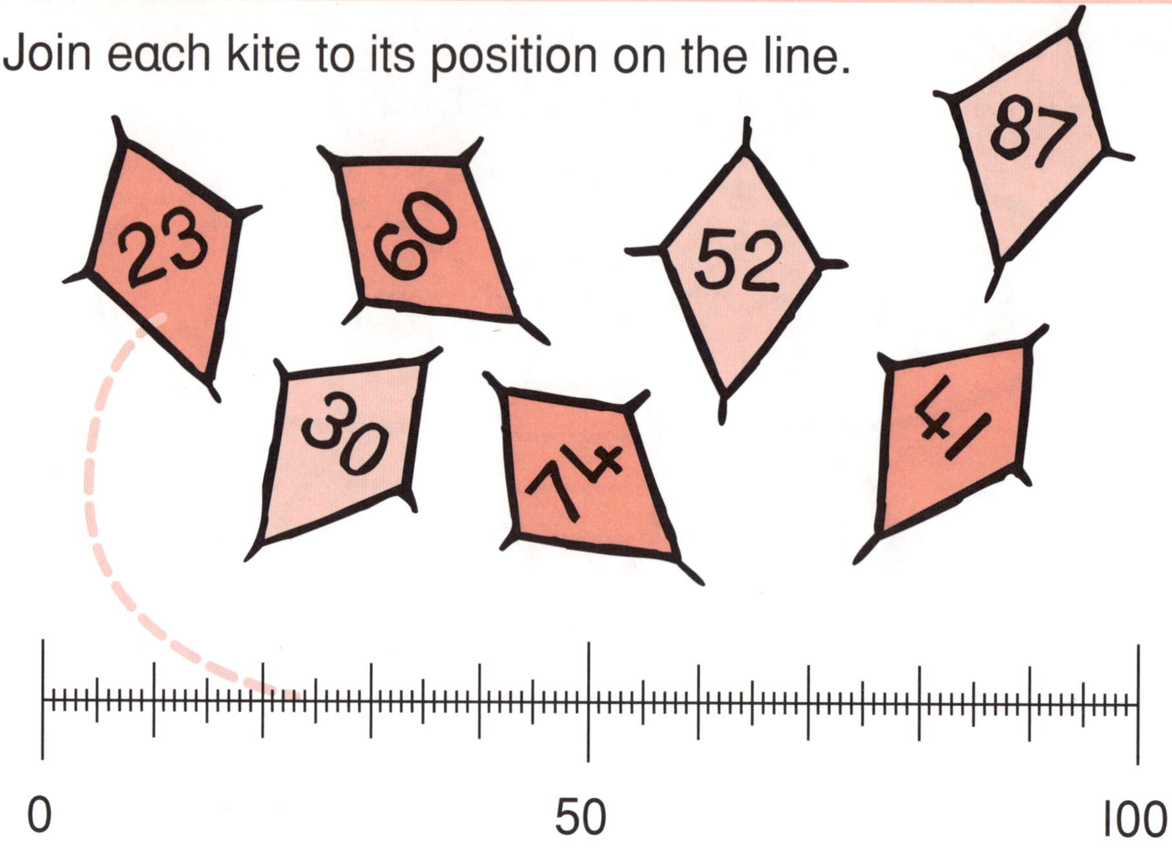

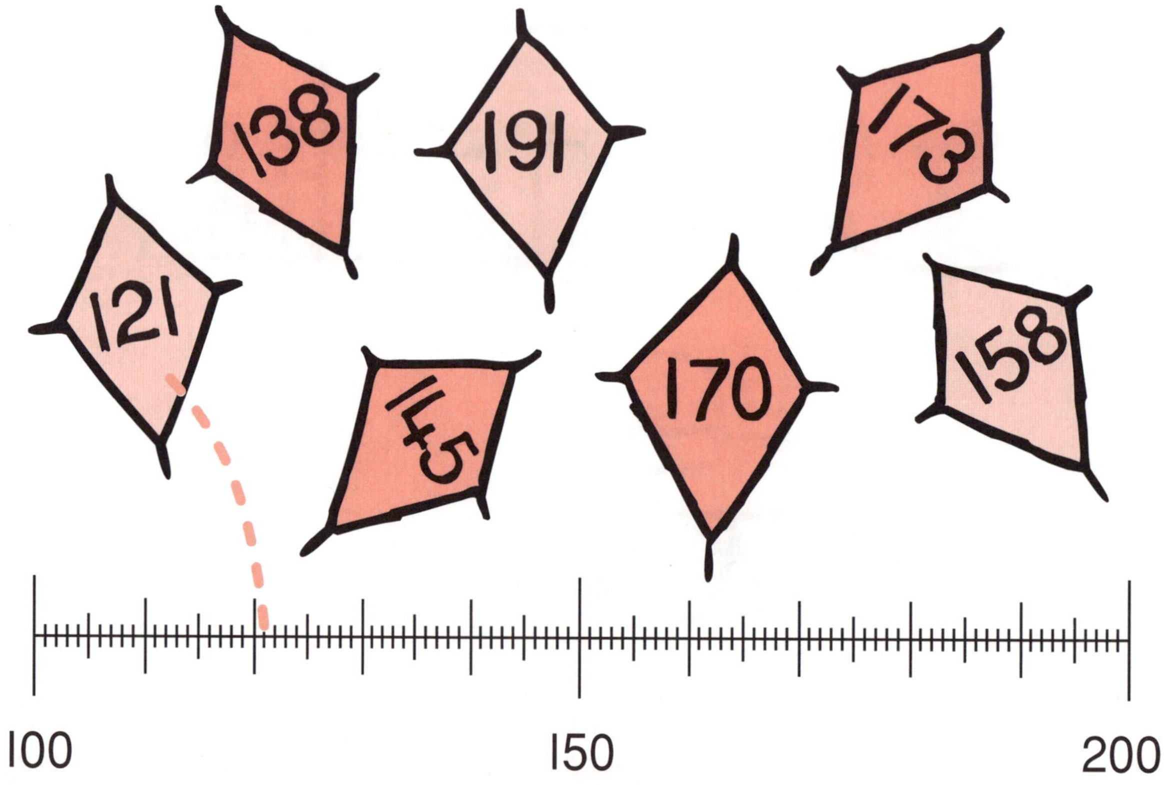

0 50 100

100 150 200

 Younger children may need help with this activity. Perhaps you could look at the divisions on a tape measure first.

Mathematics

 To recognise and name cubes, cuboids and spheres.

Shapes

Colour the shapes:

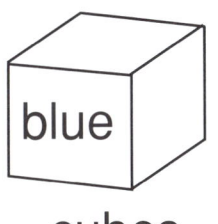
cubes

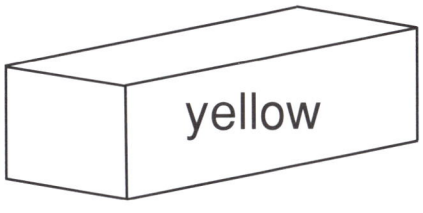
cuboids

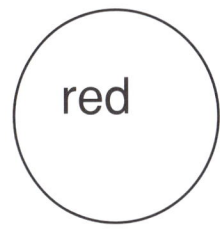
spheres

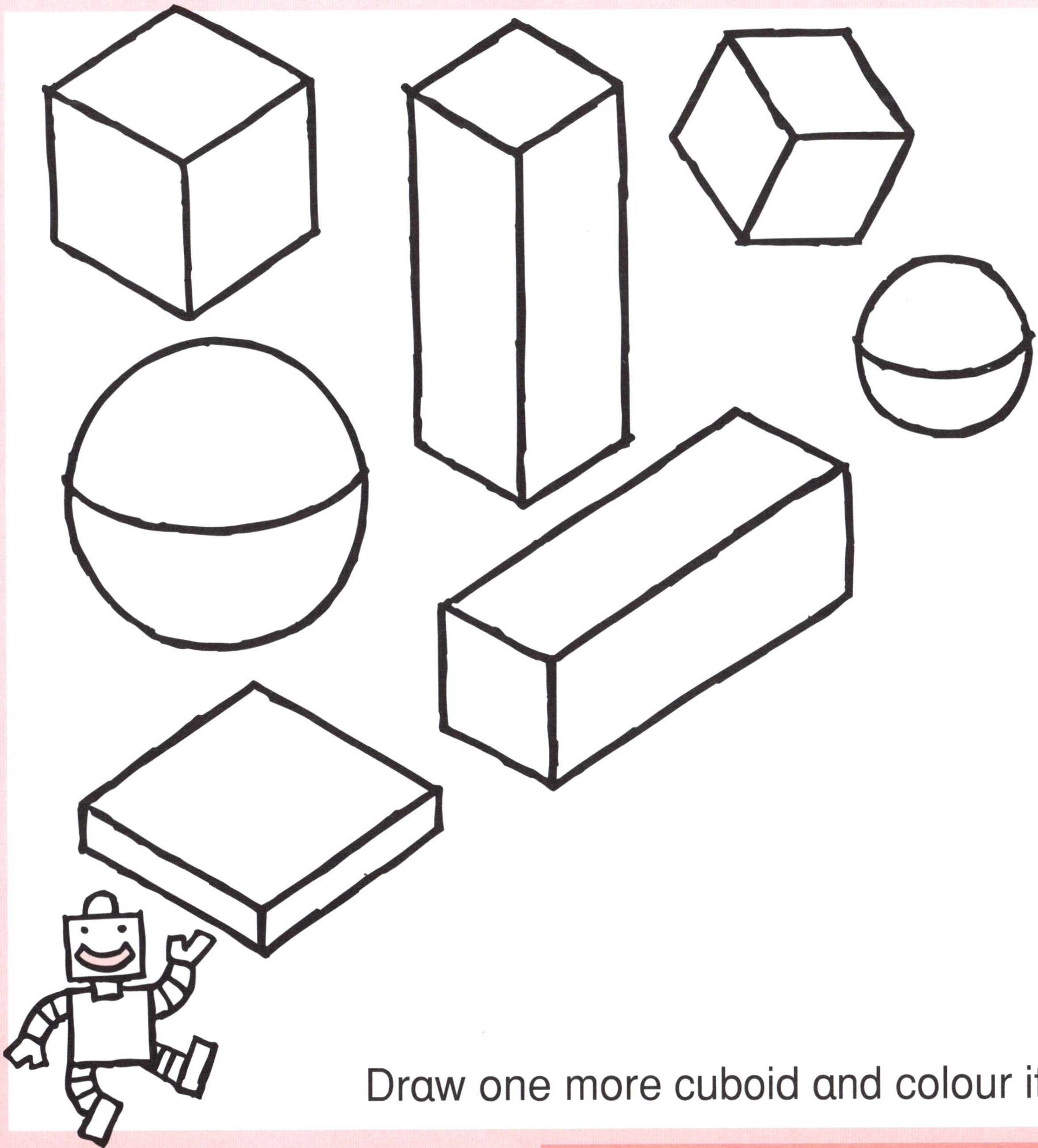

Draw one more cuboid and colour it.

 Point out 3-D shapes in the home, e.g. food packaging and furniture.

31

Mathematics

Shapes

 To recognise and name cylinders, cones and pyramids.

Colour the shapes:

      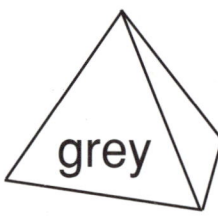

cylinders   cones   pyramids

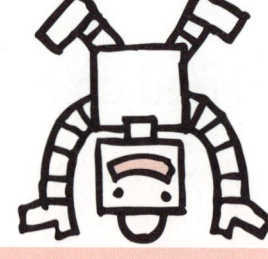 Draw one more cone and colour it.

32